W9-AQI-465

Michael Jordan

By Lisa Wade McCormick

Reading Consultant
Cecilia Minden-Cupp, PhD
Former Director of the Language and Literacy Program
Harvard Graduate School of Education
Cambridge, Massachusetts

Children's Press®
A Division of Scholastic Inc.
New York   Toronto   London   Auckland   Sydney
Mexico City   New Delhi   Hong Kong
Danbury, Connecticut

Designer: Herman Adler Design
Photo Researcher: Caroline Anderson
The photo on the cover shows Michael Jordan.
All photographs printed with permission of Michael Jordan & Estee Portnoy/
SFX Sports Group.

Library of Congress Cataloging-in-Publication Data

McCormick, Lisa Wade, 1961–
  Michael Jordan / by Lisa Wade McCormick.
    p. cm. — (Rookie biographies)
  Includes index.
  ISBN-10: 0-516-29843-7 (lib. bdg.)   0-516-27303-5 (pbk.)
  ISBN-13: 978-0-516-29843-6 (lib. bdg.)   978-0-516-27303-7 (pbk.)
  1. Jordan, Michael, 1963—Juvenile literature. 2. Basketball players—United
States—Biography—Juvenile literature. I. Title. II. Rookie biography
  GV884.J67M372 2006
  796.323092—dc22   2005030086

CHILDREN'S PRESS, and ROOKIE BIOGRAPHIES®, and associated
logos are trademarks and/or registered trademarks of Scholastic Library
Publishing. SCHOLASTIC and associated logos are trademarks and/or
registered trademarks of Scholastic Inc.
1 2 3 4 5 6 7 8 9 10 R 16 15 14 13 12 11 10 09 08 07

Can you make magic by simply shooting a basket? Michael Jordan seemed to do something magical every time he played basketball.

Jordan flew. He floated.
He soared.

Jordan's nickname is Air Jordan because of his amazing moves on the basketball court. Jordan was one of basketball's greatest players.

Michael Jeffery Jordan was born on February 17, 1963, in Brooklyn, New York.

His family moved to Wilmington, North Carolina, when he was very young. Jordan shared a home with his parents, two brothers, and two sisters.

Jordan with his parents in 1986

The Cape Fear Museum in Wilmington, North
Carolina, displays items from Jordan's younger years.

Jordan loved sports from the time he was a little boy. He decided to try out for the varsity basketball team when he was a sophomore in high school. Varsity teams are schools' top athletic teams.

Jordan wasn't picked at first, but he didn't give up. He practiced even harder, and he made the team the next year.

In 1981, Jordan started college at the University of North Carolina (UNC) in Chapel Hill, North Carolina.

Jordan attended UNC (above) from 1981 to 1984.

Jordan (right) playing for the Tar Heels in 1982

Jordan played with the Tar Heels, UNC's basketball team. He was named the top player in college basketball in both 1983 and 1984.

Jordan left UNC in 1984 to play professional basketball with the National Basketball Association (NBA).

He became the star player with a basketball team from Chicago. This team was the Chicago Bulls.

Jordan (second from left) during his first year with the Chicago Bulls

Jordan holding a trophy from the 1992 NBA championship

Jordan became world-famous during his time with the Bulls. He jumped higher than other players. He spun faster. He scored more points.

Jordan helped the Bulls win three NBA championships from 1990 to 1993.

Jordan decided to leave basketball in 1993. He wanted to spend more time with his family.

He also wanted to try playing professional baseball. Jordan played baseball for Alabama's Birmingham Barons in 1994.

Jordan during a game with the Birmingham Barons in 1994

Jordan scoring a basket for the Chicago Bulls in 1995

Jordan returned to basketball in 1995. He rejoined the Bulls and helped them win three more NBA championships. Jordan left basketball again in 1998.

In 2000, Jordan returned to the basketball court. This time, he played with a team in Washington, D.C., called the Washington Wizards.

Jordan playing for the Washington Wizards in 2002

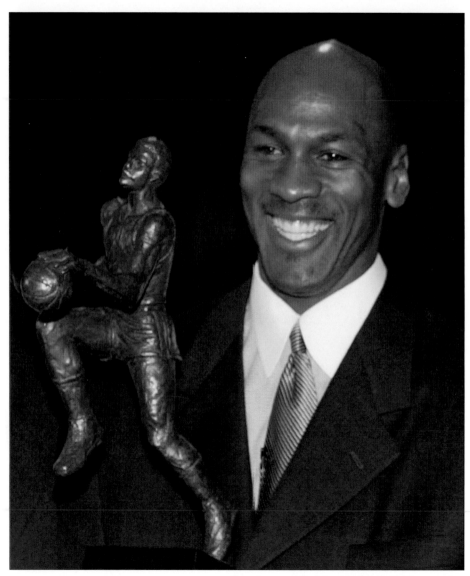

Jordan with his 1996 MVP trophy

Jordan played his last NBA game on April 16, 2003.
He was forty years old.

The NBA named Jordan its Most Valuable Player (MVP) five times. He still has one of the best records in NBA history.

Jordan also played on two U.S. Olympic basketball teams in 1984 and 1992. His team won a gold medal each time.

Jordan (center) with the winning Olympic basketball team in 1992

Jordan with members of a high school basketball team in Beijing, China, in 2004

Now, Jordan sometimes trains people in special basketball camps. He also spends time with his wife and three children.

Jordan has proven to fans everywhere that you can make magic happen if you work hard.

Words You Know

Chicago Bulls

Michael Jordan

Most Valuable Player

NBA Championship

University of North
Carolina

U.S. Olympics

Index

About the Author

Lisa Wade McCormick is a children's book author and award-winning journalist. She lives in Kansas City, Missouri, with her husband, Dave, and their two children, Wade and Madison. Lisa and her family like shooting hoops, and her son hopes to play in the NBA or Major League Baseball someday.

Photo Credits

Photographs © 2007: AP/Wide World Photos: 3, 30 top right (Mary Altaffer), 28 (Greg Baker), 24, 30 bottom (Charles Bennett), 12 (Bob Jordan), 27, 31 bottom right (Susan Ragan), 4 (John Swart); Courtesy of Cape Fear Museum of History and Science, Wilmington, NC: 8; Corbis Images/Darren Carroll/Duomo: cover; Getty Images: 16, 31 top (Andrew D. Bernstein/NBA), 20, 30 top left (Andy Hayt/NBA), 7 (Buck Miller/Time & Life Pictures), 19 (Patrick Murphy-Racey/Time & Life Pictures), 23 (Tony Ranze/AFP), 15 (Rick Stewart); Index Stock Imagery/Chip Henderson: 11, 31 bottom left.